A CALL FOR FREEDOM

A CALL FOR FREEDOM

BRYAN CURTIS, Editor

RUTLEDGE HILL PRESS™

Nashville, Tennessee

A DIVISION OF THOMAS NELSON, INC.
www.ThomasNelson.com

Published by Rutledge Hill Press,
a division of Thomas Nelson, Inc., P.O. Box 141000,
Nashville, Tennessee 37214.

Photos on pages 21, 57, 75 and 93 courtesy of Library of Congress. Photo on page 39, White House photo by Eric Draper. Photo on page 111 courtesy of the Ronald Reagan Presidential Library.

Design by Gore Studio Inc.

Library of Congress Cataloging-in-Publication Data

A call for freedom / Bryan Curtis, editor.
p. cm.
ISBN 1-4016-0005-0
1. Presidents—United States—Quotations. 2. Liberty—Quotations, maxims, etc. 3. United States—Politics and government—Quotations, maxims, etc. I. Curtis, Bryan.
E176.1 C185 2002
323.44—dc21 2002002040

Printed in the United States of America

02 03 04 05 06 — 5 4 3 2 1

To my niece, Paige Sims

I hope you will always cherish your freedoms
and use that big heart you were blessed with
to help others not as lucky as you.

Preface

"We believed then and now there are no limits to growth and human progress when men and women are free to follow their dreams." These words from President Reagan underscore the importance every man, woman, and child in America should place upon being free. As Americans, we enjoy the freedom to make decisions about our own lives, the freedom to practice the religion of our choice, the freedom to communicate what we think—whether through speaking or through writing—and the freedom to pursue any goal we can set.

The freedoms we enjoy were paid for by many courageous men and women who stood up for what they believed in—soldiers who fought on battlefields to protect this great nation; activists who, in courtrooms and on buses and in schools, fought ignorance and prejudice to ensure the civil rights of each and every American; and trailblazers who bravely ventured out into uncharted waters and lands so that others could enjoy a richer and happier life.

As you read this collection of presidential quotations, which celebrates freedoms of every kind, I hope you take a moment to thank those who have made sacrifices to maintain the liberty that has enriched your life. I also hope that you think about what you yourself can do to make not only this nation but the entire world a freer, better place to live. We should all take to heart the words of President Ford: "America will remain strong and united, but its strength will remain dedicated to the safety and sanity of the entire family of man, as well as to our own precious freedom."

America is best described by one word, freedom.

—Dwight D. Eisenhower

Through much of the last century, America's faith in freedom and democracy was a rock in a raging sea. Now it is a seed upon the wind, taking root in many nations.

—George W. Bush

Those who deny freedom deserve it not for themselves; and, under a just God, cannot long retain it.

—ABRAHAM LINCOLN

Let every nation know, whether it wishes us well or ill, we shall pay any price, bear any burden, meet any hardship, support any friend, oppose any foe, to assure the survival and success of liberty.

—JOHN F. KENNEDY

Our American values are not luxuries but necessities—not the salt in our bread but the bread itself. Our common vision of a free and just society is our greatest source of cohesion at home and strength abroad—greater than the bounty of our material blessings.

—Jimmy Carter

The American people stand firm in the faith which has inspired this Nation from the beginning. We believe that all men have a right to equal justice under law and equal opportunity to share in the common good. We believe that all men have the right to freedom of thought and expression. We believe that all men are created equal because they are created in the image of God.

—Harry S. Truman

Liberty, when it begins to take root, is a plant of rapid growth.

—George Washington

Peace is more than just the absence of war. True peace is justice. True peace is freedom. And true peace dictates the recognition of human rights.

—Ronald Reagan

Liberty must be allowed to work out its natural results; and these will, ere long, astonish the world.

—JAMES BUCHANAN

I am going to build the kind of nation that President Roosevelt hoped for, President Truman worked for, and President Kennedy died for.

—LYNDON B. JOHNSON

The welfare of our country is the great object to which our cares and efforts ought to be directed—and I shall derive great satisfaction from a co-operation with you, in the pleasing though arduous task of ensuring to our fellow citizens the blessings which they have a right to expect from a free and equal government.

—George Washington

The God who gave us life, gave us liberty at the same time: the hand of force may destroy, but cannot disjoin them.

—Thomas Jefferson

Liberty, according to my metaphysics, is an intellectual quality; an attribute that belongs neither to fate nor chance.

—John Adams

We stand today upon an eminence which overlooks a hundred years of national life—a century crowded with perils, but crowned with the triumphs of liberty and law.

—James A. Garfield

I would rather belong to a poor nation that was free than to a rich nation that had ceased to be in love with liberty. But we shall not be poor if we love liberty, because the nation that loves liberty truly sets every man free to do his best and be his best, and that means the release of all the splendid energies of a great people who can think for themselves. A nation of employees cannot be free any more than a nation of employers can be.

—Woodrow Wilson

We must ever mandate the principle that the people of this continent alone have the right to decide their own destiny.

—James K. Polk

No arsenal or no weapon in the arsenals of the world is so formidable as the will and moral courage of free men and women.

—Ronald Reagan

The Almighty God has blessed our land in many ways. He has given our people stout hearts and strong arms with which to strike mighty blows for freedom and truth. He has given to our country a faith which has become the hope of all peoples in an anguished world.

—FRANKLIN D. ROOSEVELT

Franklin D. Roosevelt signing the declaration of war against Japan on December 8, 1941.

Yesterday the greatest question was decided which was ever debated in America; and a greater perhaps never was, nor never will be, decided among men. A resolution was passed without one dissenting colony, that those United Colonies are, and of right ought to be, free and independent states.

—JOHN ADAMS

Order without liberty and liberty without order are equally destructive.

—THEODORE ROOSEVELT

We here highly resolve that these dead shall not have died in vain, that this nation under God shall have a new birth of freedom, and that government of the people, by the people, for the people shall not perish from the earth.

—ABRAHAM LINCOLN

The only foundation of a free constitution is a pure virtue.

—John Adams

There are more instances of the abridgment of the freedom of the people by gradual and silent encroachments of those in power than by violent and sudden usurpation.

—James Madison

To those new States whom we welcome to the ranks of the free, we pledge our word that one form of colonial control shall have not passed away merely to be replaced by a far more iron tyranny. We shall not always expect to find them supporting our view. But we shall always hope to find them strongly supporting their own freedom—and to remember that, in the past, those who foolishly sought power by riding the back of the tiger ended up inside.

—John F. Kennedy

The Constitution is the bedrock of all our freedoms; guard and cherish it; keep honor and order in your own house; and the republic will endure.

—Gerald Ford

The tree of liberty must be refreshed from time to time with the blood of patriots and tyrants. It is its natural manure.

—Thomas Jefferson

In the light of this equality, we know that the virtues most cherished by free people—love of truth, pride of work, devotion to country—all are treasures equally precious in the lives of the most humble and of the most exalted.

—Dwight D. Eisenhower

Liberty cannot be preserved without a general knowledge among the people.

—John Adams

If we fail now, then we will have forgotten in abundance what we learned in hardship: that democracy rests on faith, freedom asks more than it gives, and the judgment of God is harshest on those who are most favored.

—Lyndon B. Johnson

America has continued to rise through every age against every challenge, a people of great works and greater possibilities, who have always, always found the wisdom and strength to come together as one nation, to widen the circle of opportunity, to deepen the meaning of freedom to form that more perfect union.

—Bill Clinton

There can be no real peace while one American is dying someplace in the world for the rest of us. We are at war with the most dangerous enemy that has ever faced mankind in his long climb from the swamp to the stars, and it has been said if we lost that war, and in doing so lost this way of freedom of ours, history will record with the greatest astonishment that those who had the most to lose did the least to prevent its happening. . . . If we lose freedom here, there is no place to escape to. This is the last stand on Earth.

—Ronald Reagan

Only our individual faith in freedom can keep us free.

—DWIGHT D. EISENHOWER

We know what works: freedom works. We know what's right: freedom is right. We know how to secure a more just and prosperous life for man on earth: through free markets, free speech, free elections and the exercise of free will unhampered by the state.

—GEORGE BUSH

Steadfast in our faith in the Almighty, we will advance toward a world where man's freedom is secure.

—Harry S. Truman

If it be the pleasure of Heaven that my country shall require the poor offering of my life, the victim shall be ready. . . . But while I do live, let me have a country, or at least the hope of a country, and that a free country.

—John Adams

In this great nation there is but one order, that of the people, whose power, by a peculiarly happy improvement of the representative principle, is transferred from them, without impairing in the slightest degree their sovereignty, to bodies of their own creation, and to persons elected by themselves, in the full extent necessary for all the purposes of free, enlightened and efficient government.

—James Monroe

Many men die, but the fabrics of free institutions remain unshaken.

—Chester A. Arthur

Let it never be said that because of our failure to present adequately the aims and ideals of freedom, others chose the often irreversible path of dictatorship. Let us speak less of the threat of communism and more of the promise of freedom. Let us adopt as our primary objective not the defeat of communism but the victory of plenty over want, of health over disease, of freedom over tyranny.

—RICHARD M. NIXON

Today, a generation raised in the shadows of the Cold War assumes new responsibilities in a world warmed by the sunshine of freedom but threatened by still ancient hatreds and new plagues.

—BILL CLINTON

The American dream is not that every man must be level with every other man. The American dream is that every man must be free to become whatever God intends he should become.

—RONALD REAGAN

It is universally admitted that a well-instructed people alone can be a permanently free people.

—James Madison

The American continents . . . by the free and independent condition which they have assumed and maintain, are henceforth not to be considered as subjects for future colonization by any European power.

—James Monroe

Unity . . . Resolve . . . Freedom. These are the hallmarks of the American spirit. Freedom and fear are now at war, and the strength of a nation relies on the resolve and determination of its people. Our nation—this generation—will lift a dark threat of violence for our people and our future. We will rally the world to this cause by our efforts, by our courage. We will not tire, we will not falter, and we will not fail.

—George W. Bush

Without union, our independence and liberty would never have been achieved; without union they never can be maintained.

—Andrew Jackson

Posterity—you will never know how much it has cost my generation to preserve your freedom. I hope you will make good use of it.

—John Quincy Adams

Freedom is one of the deepest and noblest aspirations of the human spirit. People, worldwide, hunger for the right of self-determination, for those inalienable rights that make for human dignity and progress.

—Ronald Reagan

This fact defines the meaning of this day. We are summoned by this honored and historic ceremony to witness more than the act of one citizen swearing his oath of service, in the presence of God. We are called as a people to give testimony in the sight of the world to our faith that the future shall belong to the free.

—Dwight D. Eisenhower

Let us therefore animate and encourage each other, and show the world that a free man contending for his liberty on his own ground, is superior to any slavish mercenary on earth.

—George Washington

Liberty without learning is always in peril and learning without liberty is always in vain.

—John F. Kennedy

Ours is a constitutional freedom where the popular will is the law supreme and minorities are sacredly protected.

—Warren G. Harding

Peace, above all things, is to be desired, but blood must sometimes be spilled to obtain it on equable and lasting terms.

—Andrew Jackson

Great nations of the world are moving toward democracy through the door to freedom. Men and women of the world move toward free markets through the door to prosperity. The people of the world agitate for free expression and free thought through the door to the moral and intellectual satisfactions that only liberty allows.

—George Bush

In a free society art is not a weapon. . . . Artists are not engineers of the soul.

—John F. Kennedy

Let us remember that revolutions do not always establish freedom. Our own free institutions were not the offspring of our Revolution. They existed before.

—Millard Fillmore

It is a source of gratification and of encouragement to me to observe that the great result of this experiment upon the theory of human rights has at the close of that generation by which it was formed been crowned with success equal to the most sanguine expectations of its founders. Union, justice, tranquility, the common defense, the general welfare, and the blessings of liberty—all have been promoted by the Government under which we have lived.

—John Quincy Adams

I believe that communism is another sad, bizarre chapter in human history whose last pages even now are being written. I believe this because the source of our strength in the quest for human freedom is not material, but spiritual. And because it knows no limitation, it must terrify and ultimately triumph over those who would enslave their fellow man.

—Ronald Reagan

There is a price which is too great to pay for peace, and that price can be put in one word. One cannot pay the price of self-respect.

—Woodrow Wilson

All free governments are managed by the combined wisdom and folly of the people.

—JAMES A GARFIELD

Above all things I hope the education of the common people will be attended to, convinced that on their good sense we may rely with the most security for the preservation of a due degree of liberty.

—THOMAS JEFFERSON

I shall have liberty to think for myself without molesting others or being molested myself.

—John Adams

The durability of free speech and free press rests on the simple concept that it search for the truth and tell the truth.

—Herbert Hoover

In the election of 1860, Abraham Lincoln said the question was whether this Nation could exist half slave or half free. In the election of 1960, and with the world around us, the question is whether the world will exist half slave or half free, whether it will move in the direction of freedom, in the direction of the road that we are taking, or whether it will move in the direction of slavery.

—John F. Kennedy

God gave us Lincoln and liberty. Let's fight for both.

—Ulysses S. Grant

It is the task of statesmanship to mold, to balance, and to integrate these and other forces, new and old, within the principles of our democratic system—ever aiming toward the supreme goals of our free society.

—Dwight D. Eisenhower

America is a nation full of good fortune, with so much to be grateful for. But we are not spared from suffering. In every generation, the world has produced enemies of human freedom. They have attacked America, because we are freedom's home and defender. And the commitment of our fathers is now the calling of our time.

—George W. Bush

The only maxim of a free government ought to be to trust no man living with power to endanger the public liberty.

—JOHN ADAMS

It shall be my first and highest duty to preserve unimpaired the free institutions under which we live and transmit them to those who shall succeed me in their full force and vigor.

—JOHN TYLER

I would rather be exposed to the inconveniences attending too much liberty than those attending too small a degree of it.

—Thomas Jefferson

America today is a proud, free nation, decent and civil, a place we cannot help but love.

—George Bush

No union exists between church and state, and perfect freedom of opinion is guaranteed to all sects and creeds.

—James K. Polk

I am exceedingly anxious that this Union, the Constitution, and the liberties of the people shall be perpetuated in accordance with the original idea for which that struggle was made, and I shall be most happy indeed if I shall be a humble instrument in the hands of the Almighty, and of this, His most chosen people, for perpetuating the object of that great struggle.

—ABRAHAM LINCOLN

Statesmen may plan and speculate for liberty, but it is religion and morality alone which can establish the principles upon which freedom can securely stand.

—JOHN ADAMS

We have no desire to be the world's policeman. But America does want to be the world's peacemaker.

—JIMMY CARTER

Liberty is to faction what air is to fire, an ailment without it instantly expires. But it could not be less folly to abolish liberty, which is essential to political life, because it nourishes faction, than it would be to wish the annihilation of air, which is essential to animal life, because it imparts to fire its destructive agency.

—James Madison

America will remain strong and united, but its strength will remain dedicated to the safety and sanity of the entire family of man, as well as to our own precious freedom.

—GERALD FORD

You must remember, my fellow citizens, that eternal vigilance by the people is the price of liberty, and that you must pay the price if you wish to secure the blessing.

—Andrew Jackson

That the blessings of liberty which our Constitution secures may be enjoyed alike by minorities and majorities, the Executive has been wisely invested with a qualified veto upon the act of the Legislature.

—James K. Polk

We preach freedom around the world, and we mean it, and we cherish our freedom here at home, but are we to say to the world, and much more importantly, to each other that this is the land of the free except for the Negroes; that we have no second-class citizens except for the Negroes; that we have no class or caste system, no ghettoes, no master race except with respect to Negroes?

—John F. Kennedy

Liberty is to the collective body, what health is to every individual body. Without health, no pleasure can be tasted by man, without liberty, no happiness can be enjoyed by society.

—THOMAS JEFFERSON

Let us by all wise and constitutional measures promote intelligence among the people as the best means of preserving our liberties.

—JAMES MONROE

The march of freedom and democracy . . . will leave Marxism-Leninism on the ash heap of history as it has left other tyrannies which stifle the freedom and muzzle the self-expression of the people.

—Ronald Reagan

The war has proved . . . that our free government, like other free governments, though slow in its early movements, acquires, in its progress, a force proportioned to its freedom.

—James Madison

True individual freedom cannot exist without economic security and independence. People who are hungry and out of a job are the stuff of which dictatorships are made.

—Franklin D. Roosevelt

Tonight, we are a country awakened to danger and called to defend freedom. Our grief has turned to anger and anger to resolution. Whether we bring our enemies to justice or bring justice to our enemies, justice will be done.

—George W. Bush

All free people ought not only to be armed but disciplined; to which end a uniform and well-digested plan is requisite.

—George Washington

This vision still grips the imagination of the world. But we know that democracy is always an unfinished creation. Each generation must renew its foundations. Each generation must discover the meaning of this hallowed vision in the light of its own modern challenges. For this generation, ours, life is nuclear survival; liberty is human rights; the pursuit of happiness is a planet whose resources are devoted to the physical and spiritual nourishment of its inhabitants.

—Jimmy Carter

Conformity is the jailer of freedom and enemy of growth.

—John F. Kennedy

Public virtue is the vital spirit of republics, and history proved that when this has decayed and the love of money has usurped its place, although the forms of free government may remain for a season, the substance has departed forever.

—James Buchanan

No government ought to be without censors, and where the press is free, no one ever will.

—Thomas Jefferson

In a free government the security for civil rights must be the same as for religious rights. It consists in that one case in the multiplicity of interest, and the other in the multiplicity of sects.

—James Madison

Democracy belongs to us all, and freedom is like a beautiful kite that can go higher and higher with the breeze.

—George Bush

We cannot overestimate the fervent love of liberty, the intelligent courage, and the sum of common sense with which our fathers made the great experiment of self-government.

—James A. Garfield

The house we hope to build is not for my generation but for yours. It is your future that matters. And I hope that when you are my age, you will be able to say as I have been able to say: We lived in freedom. We lived lives that were a statement, not an apology.

—Ronald Reagan

Americans, indeed all freemen, remember that in the final choice, a soldier's pack is not so heavy a burden as a prisoner's chains.

—DWIGHT D. EISENHOWER

Dwight D. Eisenhower giving orders to American paratroopers in England before the invasion of Normandy on June 6, 1944.

I deem the present occasion sufficiently important and solemn to justify me in expressing to my fellow citizens a profound reverence for the Christian religion and a thorough conviction that sound morals, religious liberty, and a just sense of religious responsibility are essentially connected with all true and lasting happiness; and to that good Being who has blessed us by the gifts of civil and religious freedom, who watched over and prospered the labors of our fathers and has hitherto preserved to us institutions far exceeding in excellence those of any other people, let us unite in fervently commending every interest of our beloved country in all future time.

—WILLIAM HENRY HARRISON

History does not long entrust the care of freedom to the weak or the timid.

—Dwight D. Eisenhower

Those who desire to give up freedom in order to gain security, will not have, nor do they deserve, either one.

—Thomas Jefferson

We must support our rights or lose our character, and with it, perhaps our liberties.

—James Monroe

We've defeated freedom's enemies before, and we will defeat them again. We have refused to live in a state of panic or in a state of denial. There is a difference between being alert and being intimidated and this great nation will never be intimidated.

—George W. Bush

Two centuries ago our nation's birth was a milestone in the long quest for freedom, but the bold and brilliant dream which excited the founders of our nation still awaits its consummation. I have no new dream to set forth today, but rather urge a fresh faith in the old dream.

—Jimmy Carter

Let them revere nothing but religion, morality, and liberty.

—John Adams

Democracy is worth dying for, because it's the most deeply honorable form of government ever devised by man.

—Ronald Reagan

You know, when the framers finished crafting our Constitution in Philadelphia, Benjamin Franklin stood in Independence Hall and he reflected on the carving of the sun that was on the back of a chair he saw. The sun was low on the horizon. So he said this—he said, "I've often wondered whether that sun was rising or setting. Today," Franklin said, " I have the happiness to know it's a rising sun." Today, because each succeeding generation of Americans has kept the fire of freedom burning brightly, lighting those frontiers of possibility, we all still bask in the glow and the warmth of Mr. Franklin's sun.

—Bill Clinton

The nation's honor is dearer than the nation's comfort; yes, than the nation's life itself.

—Woodrow Wilson

Our greatest happiness does not depend on the condition of life in which chance has placed us, but it is always the result of a good conscience, good health, occupation, and freedom in all just pursuits.

—Thomas Jefferson

America was not built on fear. America was built on courage, on imagination and an unbeatable determination to do the job at hand.

—HARRY S. TRUMAN

Conceiving the defense of freedom, like freedom itself, to be one and indivisible, we hold all continents and peoples in equal regard and honor. We reject any insinuation that one race or another, one people or another, is in any sense inferior or expendable.

—DWIGHT D. EISENHOWER

There is nothing stable but Heaven and the Constitution.

—James Buchanan

The fundamental precept of liberty is toleration. We can not permit any inquisition either within or without the law or apply any religious test to the holding of office. The mind of America must be forever free.

—Calvin Coolidge

In the future days which we seek to make secure, we look forward to a world founded upon four essential human freedoms. The first is freedom of speech and expression—everywhere in the world. The second is freedom of every person to worship God in his own way—everywhere in the world. The third freedom is from want . . . —everywhere in the world. The fourth is freedom from fear . . . —anywhere in the world. The world order which we seek is the cooperation of free countries, working together in a friendly, civilized society. This nation has placed its destiny in the hands, heads and hearts of its millions of free men and women and its faith in freedom under the guidance of God. Freedom means the supremacy of human rights everywhere. Our support goes to those who struggle to gain those rights and keep them. Our strength is our unity of purpose. To that high concept, there can be no end save victory.

—Franklin D. Roosevelt

The approbation implied by your suffrage is a great consolation to me for the past, and my future solicitude will be to retain the good opinion of those who have bestowed it in advance, to conciliate that of others by doing them all the good in my power, and to be instrumental to the happiness and freedom of all.

—George Washington

The best road to progress is freedom's road.

—John F. Kennedy

Love of liberty means the guarding of every resource that makes freedom possible—from the sanctity of our families and the wealth of our soil to the genius of our scientists.

—Dwight D. Eisenhower

My fellow citizens of the world: ask not what America will do for you, but what together we can do for the freedom of man.

—John F. Kennedy

We will stand mighty for peace and freedom, and maintain a strong defense against terror and destruction. Our children will sleep free from the threat of nuclear, chemical or biological weapons.

—Bill Clinton

This is not, however, just America's fight. And what is at stake is not just America's freedom. This is the world's fight. This is civilization's fight. This is the fight of all who believe in progress and pluralism, tolerance and freedom.

—George W. Bush

There is something back of there, entwining itself more closely about the human heart. That something is the principle of "Liberty to all"—the principle that clears the path for all, gives hope to all, and, by consequence, enterprise and industry to all.

—Abraham Lincoln

Abraham Lincoln meets with Soujourner Truth at the White House on October 29, 1864.

The time is now and near at hand which must probably determine whether Americans are to be freemen or slaves; whether they are to have property they can call their own; whether their houses and farms are to be pillaged and destroyed, and themselves consigned to a state of wretchedness from which no human efforts will deliver them. The fate of unborn millions will now depend, under God, on courage and conduct of this army. Our cruel and relenting enemy leaves us the only choice of brave resistance, or the most abject submission. We have, therefore, to resolve to conquer or die.

—George Washington

No people can live to itself alone. The unity of all who dwell in freedom is their only sure defense.

—DWIGHT D. EISENHOWER

I will not forget the wound to our country and those who inflicted it. I will not yield, I will not rest, I will not relent in waging this struggle for freedom and security for the American people.

—GEORGE W. BUSH

Democracy is not dying. We know it because we have seen it revive—and grow. We know it cannot die—because it is built on the unhampered initiative of individual men and women joined together in a common enterprise—an enterprise undertaken and carried through by the free expression of a free majority.

—Franklin D. Roosevelt

Today we are committed to a worldwide struggle to promote and protect the rights of all who wish to be free.

—John F. Kennedy

As for the enemies of freedom, those who are potential adversaries, they will be reminded that peace is the highest aspiration of the American people. We will negotiate for it, sacrifice for it; we will not surrender for it—now or ever.

—Ronald Reagan

But our greatest strength is the power of our ideas, which are still new in many lands. Across the world, we see them embraced—and we rejoice. Our hopes, our hearts, our hands, are with those on every continent who are building democracy and freedom. Their cause is America's cause.

—BILL CLINTON

I contend that the strongest of all governments is that which is most free.

—William Henry Harrison

Liberty is the great parent of science and virtue; and a nation will be great in both in proportion as it is free.

—THOMAS JEFFERSON

We feel this moral strength because we know that we are not helpless prisoners of history. We are free men. We shall remain free, never to be proven guilty of the one capital offense against freedom, a lack of staunch faith.

—DWIGHT D. EISENHOWER

And yet we all understand what it is—the spirit—the faith of America. It is the product of centuries. It was born in the multitudes of those who came from many lands—some of high degree, but mostly plain people, who sought here, early and late, to find freedom more freely.

—Franklin D. Roosevelt

We observe today not a victory of a party, but a celebration of freedom—symbolizing an end, as well as a beginning—signifying renewal, as well as change. For I have sworn before you and Almighty God the same solemn oath our forebears prescribed nearly a century and three quarters ago.

—John F. Kennedy

Posterity, you will never know how much it cost the present generation to preserve your freedom. I hope you will make good use of it. If you do not, I shall repent in heaven that ever I took half the pains to preserve it.

—John Adams

Genius is free to announce its inventions and discoveries, and the hand is free to accomplish whatever the head conceives not incompatible with the rights of a fellow-being.

—James K. Polk

The world has never had a good definition of the word liberty, and the American people, just now, are much in want of one. We all declare for liberty; but in using the same word we do not all mean the same thing. With some, the word liberty may mean for each man to do as he pleases with himself, and the product of his labor; while with others the same word may mean for some men to do as they please with other men, and the product of other men's labor. Here are two, not only different, but incompatible things, called by the same name, liberty.

—Abraham Lincoln

As long as the United States of America is determined and strong, this will not be an age of terror. This will be an age of liberty here and across the world.

—GEORGE W. BUSH

The real differences around the world today are not between Jews and Arabs; Protestants and Catholics; Muslims, Croats, and Serbs. The real differences are between those who embrace peace and those who destroy it; between those who look to the future and those who cling to the past; between those who open their arms and those who are determined to clench their fists.

—Bill Clinton

The gains in education are never really lost. Books may be burned and cities sacked, but truth, like the yearning for freedom, lives in the hearts of humble men.

—Franklin D. Roosevelt

When people talk of the freedom of writing, speaking, or thinking I cannot choose but laugh. No such thing ever existed. No such thing now exists; but I hope it will exist. But it must be hundreds of years after you and I shall write and speak no more.

—John Adams

Resistance to tyrants is obedience to God.

—Thomas Jefferson

Individual liberty is individual power, and as the power of a community is a mass compounded of individual powers, the nation which enjoys the most freedom must necessarily be in proportion to its numbers the most powerful nation.

—John Quincy Adams

If we meet our responsibilities, I think freedom will conquer. If we fail, if we fail to move ahead, if we fail to develop sufficient military and economic and social strength here in this country, then I think that the tide could begin to run against us, and I don't want historians ten years from now to say, these were the years when the tide ran out for the United States. I want them to say, these were the years when the tide came in, these were the years when the United States started to move again. That's the question before the American people, and only you can decide what you want, what you want this country to be, what you want to do with the future.

—John F. Kennedy

We believed then and now there are no limits to growth and human progress when men and women are free to follow their dreams.

—Ronald Reagan

In Europe, charters of liberty have been granted by power. America has set the example, and France has followed it, of charters of power granted by liberty.

—James Madison

Let every American, every lover of liberty, every well-wisher to his posterity, swear by the blood of the Revolution never to violate in the least particular the laws of the country, and never to tolerate their violation by others.

—Abraham Lincoln

In the long history of the world, only a few generations have been granted the role of defending freedom in its hour of maximum danger. . . . The energy, the faith, the devotion which we bring to this endeavor will light our country and all who serve it, and the glow from that fire can truly light the world.

—John F. Kennedy

The promise of America was born in the 18th century out of the bold conviction that we are all created equal. It was extended and preserved in the 19th century, when our nation spread across the continent, saved the union, and abolished the awful scourge of slavery.

—BILL CLINTON

America must remain freedom's staunchest friend, for freedom is our best ally.

—Ronald Reagan

Let those who would die for the flag on the field of battle give a better proof of their patriotism and a higher glory to their country by promoting fraternity and justice.

—Benjamin Harrison

Our reliance is the love of liberty which God has planted in our bosoms. Our defense is in the preservation of the spirit which prized liberty as the heritage of all men, in all lands, everywhere. Destroy this spirit and you have planted the seeds of despotism around your own doors. Familiarize yourselves with the chains of bondage, and you are preparing your own limbs to wear them.

—Abraham Lincoln

Peace is a daily, a weekly, a monthly process, gradually changing opinions, slowly eroding old barriers, quietly building new structures.

—JOHN F. KENNEDY

Steadfast in our purpose, we now press on. We have known freedom's price. We have shown freedom's power. And in this great conflict, my fellow Americans, we will see freedom's victory.

—GEORGE W. BUSH

The Constitution itself, plainly written as it is, the safeguard of our federative compact, the offspring of concession and compromise, binding together in the bonds of peace and union this great and increasing family of free and independent states, will be the chart by which I shall be directed.

—JAMES K. POLK

If our country does not lead the cause for freedom, it will not be led.

—George W. Bush

The ground of liberty is to be gained by inches, and we must be contented to secure what we can get from time to time and eternally press forward for what is yet to get. It takes time to persuade men to do even what is for their own good.

—Thomas Jefferson

The cost of freedom is always high, but Americans have always paid it. And one path we shall never choose, and that is the path of surrender, or submission.

—John F. Kennedy

I believe the declaration that "all men are created equal" is the great fundamental principle upon which our free institutions rest.

—Abraham Lincoln

As we renew ourselves here in our own land, we will be seen as having greater strength throughout the world. We will again be the example of freedom and a beacon of hope for those who do not now have freedom.

—Ronald Reagan

As the sword was the last resort for the preservation of our liberties, so it ought to be the first to be laid aside when those liberties are firmly established.

—George Washington

In the midst of these pleasing ideas we should be unfaithful to ourselves if we should ever lose sight of the danger to our liberties if anything partial or extraneous should infect the purity of our free, fair, virtuous and independent elections.

—John Adams

Events have brought our American democracy to new influence and new responsibilities. They will test our courage, our devotion to duty, and our concept of liberty. But I say to all men, what we have achieved in liberty, we will surpass in greater liberty.

—Harry S. Truman

May those generations whose faces we cannot yet see, whose names we may never know, say of us here that we led our beloved land into a new century with the American Dream alive for all her children; with the American promise of a more perfect union a reality for all her people; with America's bright flame of freedom spreading throughout the world.

—Bill Clinton

America did not invent human rights. In a very real sense . . . human rights invented America.

—Jimmy Carter

Freedom and fear, justice and cruelty, have always been at war, and we know that God is not neutral between them.

—George W. Bush

We will always remember. We will always be proud. We will always be prepared, so we may always be free.

—Ronald Reagan

America has been the New World in all tongues, to all peoples, not because this continent was a new-found land, but because all those who came here believed they could create upon this continent a new life—a life that should be new in freedom.

—Franklin D. Roosevelt

May the light of freedom, coming to all darkened lands, flame brightly—until at last the darkness is no more.

—Dwight D. Eisenhower

PRESIDENTIAL TERMS

1.	George Washington	1789–1797
2.	John Adams	1797–1801
3.	Thomas Jefferson	1801–1809
4.	James Madison	1809–1817
5.	James Monroe	1817–1825
6.	John Quincy Adams	1825–1829
7.	Andrew Jackson	1829–1837
8.	Martin Van Buren	1837–1841
9.	William Henry Harrison	1841
10.	John Tyler	1841–1845
11.	James K. Polk	1845–1849
12.	Zachary Taylor	1849–1850
13.	Millard Fillmore	1850–1853
14.	Franklin Pierce	1853–1857
15.	James Buchanan	1857–1861
16.	Abraham Lincoln	1861–1865
17.	Andrew Johnson	1865–1869
18.	Ulysses S. Grant	1869–1877
19.	Rutherford B. Hayes	1877–1881
20.	James A. Garfield	1881
21.	Chester A. Arthur	1881–1885
22.	Grover Cleveland	1885–1889
23.	Benjamin Harrison	1889–1893
24.	Grover Cleveland	1893–1897
25.	William McKinley	1897–1901
26.	Theodore Roosevelt	1901–1909
27.	William H. Taft	1909–1913
28.	Woodrow Wilson	1913–1921
29.	Warren G. Harding	1921–1923
30.	Calvin Coolidge	1923–1929
31.	Herbert Hoover	1929–1933
32.	Franklin D. Roosevelt	1933–1945
33.	Harry S. Truman	1945–1953
34.	Dwight D. Eisenhower	1953–1961
35.	John F. Kennedy	1961–1963
36.	Lyndon B. Johnson	1963–1969
37.	Richard M. Nixon	1969–1974
38.	Gerald Ford	1974–1977
39.	Jimmy Carter	1977–1981
40.	Ronald Reagan	1981–1989
41.	George Bush	1989–1993
42.	Bill Clinton	1993–2001
43.	George W. Bush	2001–